BLINDED BIRDS

poems by

B. Fulton Jennes

Finishing Line Press
Georgetown, Kentucky

BLINDED BIRDS

You who do not remember
passage from the other world
I tell you I could speak again: whatever
returns from oblivion returns
to find a voice

Louise Glück, "The Wild Iris"

To Mallory, who has found her voice

ACKNOWLEDGMENTS

"Silver Demon" in *The Comstock Review*
"Every Bad Thing That Ever Happened to Me" in *The Night Heron Barks*
"Black Bread," "Ghazal: For a Wild Child, Grown," and "Eating Dinner, After
You Died" in *Tupelo Quarterly*
"To Another Addict's Mother," "The Relapse," and "Hovenweep" in *Anti-Heroin Chic*

Publisher: Leah Huete de Maines
Editor: Christen Kincaid
Cover Art: *The Illustrated Book of Canaries and Cage-Birds*, by W.A.
Blakston, S. Swaysland, and A.F. Wiener in Public Domain
Author Photo: Susie Buckley
Cover Design: Elizabeth Maines McCleavy

Order online: www.finishinglinepress.com
also available on amazon.com

Author inquiries and mail orders:
Finishing Line Press
PO Box 1626
Georgetown, Kentucky 40324
USA

Table of Contents

BLINDED BIRDS

The Flemish blinded finches with fire-heated needles;
they claimed it made the birds sing more beautifully.

Lost in their world of darkness, undistracted by daylight,
song swelled in the sorry birds' breasts like prayer.

God heard and saw and did nothing, only marveled
at the loveliness of these man-crafted mutants.

He fashions blinded birds of His own, engineers
endless misinterpretations of the master genome,

experiments with alleles, entertains Himself
with quirks and tics, incapacitations, addictions.

Lean closer, God—hear voices from a world left
darkened by your whims. Our hearts are heated needles.

We will not sing for you.

SORRY (SHE SAYS)

The psychic has news from you:
She wants to say she's sorry.

No explanation offered, but none is needed.
I left home with a hope chest full of your fury.

You weren't a bad mother, just a sad one,
stymied by sorrows genetically gifted to you.

You always spoke longingly of death
as if it were on everyone's Christmas list.

No matter how many times I heard it,
it always meant the same: not enough.

My love was a broken boomerang,
unable to fell the wolves that chased you.

Where is she? I ask, ignoring the obvious: dead.
Zipping around the universe, she replies,

with her sister. She's very happy. I remember
a childhood folk song about a happy wanderer

who laughed and sang—*faleri falera, faleri falera.*
He wasn't sorry in the least.

TO AN ALLELE

Numerous research studies since the mid-1990s have linked the A1 allele—a mutation on the human D2 dopamine receptor gene—with depression and anxiety that manifest as early as infancy, severe alcoholism, ADHD, intractable PTSD, and a heightened risk of addiction to opium, cocaine, and heroin.

Diminutive despot,
maker
of all manner
of trickle-down tragedies—
birthrights
as ineludible
as red hair,
attached earlobes,
freckled skin—

chromosomal Kroni,
invisible to
the gene-tinted eye,
what ambition
drives you
to lead us into
addiction,
addled distraction,
playground despair?

Tainter of brains,
mutant hijacker
of mirth,
what God
created you in
His image,
put you in
the driver's seat,
handed you
so damn
many keys?

SILVER DEMON

She kept her carton of Pall Malls in the pantry—
a staple as dependable as the dusty flour jar
or yellow ten-pound sack of sugar.
Sometimes she'd ask me to fetch a fresh, red pack.

I'd watch her peel the cellophane seal,
tear a square opening in the silver foil, tap out
a sleek cylinder of white paper and tight tobacco,
then purse it between her eager lips.

The match would catch a sputtering blaze
and she'd transfer its glow to the cigarette's end
before wrist-flicking the flame to nothingness.
She could extinguish me with just that much ease.

She'd suck in the hot cloud of relief,
spit bits of tobacco from her tongue,
sit back and blow ghostly smoke
to the ceiling, expelling a silver demon.

The Surgeon General's warnings were new,
heralded by Walter Cronkite on the 6:30 report,
affirmed by our grade-school teachers: *Children,
don't smoke. You'll die of lung cancer.*

So once, watching her smoke, I inched closer
on my knees and whispered: *Please, Mommy,
don't die.* She froze me with a wild-eyed glare—
an unwanted interruption of ease.

But then the smoke's relief took hold
and I disappeared—a crumpled list of chores,
tossed from a car window, bouncing out of sight
in a broken rear-view mirror.

DRINKING WITH DADDY

On weeknights, the safe time ended
    when the garage door's rumble warned us
        to scatter from after-school cartoons.

Hidden from sight, we became small,
    invisible things until the balm of gin
        defused his thorny angers, made him

silent and dull at dinner. But on Sundays,
    just before the midday feast,
        the penance of church behind him,

he invited whichever of us arrived first
    on his lap to froth our upper lip
        with ephemeral endearment, sipped

from an iced pilsner glass. *Good, yes?*
    Words uttered so close to our ears that
        his yeasty exhale became our next breath.

Yes, yes! we agreed: a mouthful of what
    passed for affection—how could it not be?
        Years later, awash in hangovers, blackouts,

unquenchable longings, forever dismissed
    from his hallowed lap, I guzzled the poison
        of his legacy, drunk with the right answer.

AM I DEAD?

I.
Do all little girls
lust after Death—
the invisible friend
with all the best toys:
dirt, distance,
cool, dark depths?

I did. I invited him in
again and again,
just as my mother did,
treating him like
a visiting minister:
with reverence.
Without fear.
Expecting forgiveness.

II.
I first met Death
as I gripped the rail of my crib,
snorted back snot,
and wailed for
the harsh-handed mother
who did not want
to come for me
to come for me.

Death came.
He entered the room smiling,
looked like the colorless man
who smiled from atop
my grandmother's dresser.
And although
we were strangers then,
I felt his love
and knew that
all I had to do
was long for him
and he would
come again.

III.
My father
couldn't abide
my precocious sorrow.
What the hell
do you have
to be sad about?
he bellowed, waving
his open hand
at the shade-darkened house,
the meaningless acres.

IV.
After the little girl
who shared my name
rose from bed one night
and died, I missed
her at Sunday school,
missed her orange hair
and white-gloved hand
holding mine as we
leaned, shoulder to shoulder,
to sing *I'm gonna let it shine.*
So one Sunday afternoon,
I slipped away from
the dinner table,
retrieved the pistol
from its secret place
in my father's office,
put the barrel
to my temple,
heard-felt
the metallic click.
Then I trudged
to my father's place
at the head of the table
and asked,
Am I dead?

V.
My mother says
I was born sad,
covered head to toe
with staph boils
that festered
and oozed.
I convulsed
at the touch
of a mother's hand.

You cried nonstop for months
she says and looks away.
In silence, I ask,
Is that when you
first wanted
to flee?

VI.
A smiling baby
means
a happy mother
means
nobody wants to die.

EVERY BAD THING THAT EVER HAPPENED TO ME

happened when I was drunk,
I'll say in retrospect.

But right now, I'm 14 and three beers into
a stolen six-pack, kissing Teddy Briscoe,
whose tongue trembles and frolics
after mine, whose saliva is sweet, and who
pauses a moment to take off his glasses
and bed them in the warm grass beside us.

Music from the firehouse Teen Hop
echoes across the lake, and while we kiss,
a silent moon saunters across the sky.

For the first time in my life, I felt normal.
That's what I'll say, what we all say,
giving a speech at the AA celebration
honoring our year of sobriety.
But for now, it's truth with a capital T,
and the awakening Reward-o-Meter
in my brain is setting off alarms,
red lights, bells, applause.

When my father picks me up at the firehouse
hours later, he asks if I stayed out of trouble.
I want to tell him the truth.
I want to describe the feeling of tumblers
falling into place in a safe door,
of rockets released at last from
gravity's dark hold.

HOW I QUIT DRINKING FOR YOU

Desperate belief
on fertility-clinic tables,
amulets gripped under pillows—
when my longing for you
yielded only monthly blood,
I doubted and raged,
cursed a miserly universe.

God answered, sent a sign
as I staggered
from party to car:
a just-hatched chick,
featherless, pink, tossed
from the nest, unnoticed
on the sidewalk—
a barely discernable crunch
of frail calcium twigs.

That night, I drained
bottle after bottle
into the sink's drunken gullet,
set about building
a nest that wouldn't spill
its fragile contents,
imagined my hands,
untrembling,
able to catch
small, falling things.

MOTHER'S MILK

A weary nurse wheels you down the hall,
wailing for mother's milk.

My breasts ache with the call of you.
But as the door gapes open,

piercing the bed with sick-yellow hospital light,
I know that I will fail.

My nipples retract, refuse to surface;
your nascent tongue folds back upon itself.

We both long for what
we cannot have.

The pediatrician frowns at your declining weight,
orders me to drink beer.

For seven years, I've pushed the leaden stone of sobriety
up an interminable slope.

Here at last: a reason to let it go, let it bounce and bang
to the bottom of the cairn of prayers.

Soon, poisoned milk fills my breasts, and when you
reject my offering with a yowl,

I understand: I'll never shield you from my hunger,
never save you from your own.

POST-PARTUM PANTOUM

Dear one, I am not the nurturer you need.
These sagging sacks are filled with only emptiness.
Some god has played such cruel hormonal trickery:
I'm mortified to say, I have no milk today.

These sagging sacks are filled with only emptiness.
What kind of nourishment is blue-black nothingness?
I'm terrified to say, I have no milk today.
Please suckle on my heart—it aches to sustain you.

What kind of nourishment surpasses nothingness?
When nature fails, can love alone suffice?
Please suckle on my heart—it aches to nourish you.
Spit out the bitter sorrow that has curdled there.

So much depends on oxytocin's alchemy.
Nature fails—such cruel hormonal insufficiency.
Spit out the curdled love, the only milk I give.
I will never be the nurturer you need.

BLACK BREAD

My mother was lovely, I believed.
She wore her sadness as a gown;
it swirled around her ankles in thick ripples,
its bodice cut low across her chest to reveal
a dark crevasse between her breasts
that fractured straight to her heart,
weighted her down like the Virgin Queen,
incapacitated by hideous finery.

I spent my days alone with her.
She fed me black bread made
from black flour kept in a black canister.
It tasted like love.
She wrote the recipe on my soft skin,
instructed me to bake it for my children.

You cried the first time I fed you
a tiny morsel, mixed with something sweet
to cloak the afterbite.
Like so many things worth having,
it takes time to develop a taste
for bitterness.

You'll see me wear her gown
tomorrow and the next day.
I keep it hidden in the darkest
depths of my closet,
only put it on when you
and I are alone.

Someday, you'll think I'm lovely.
Someday, the gown will fit you.

Hush now.
Eat your bread.

ALKY MOMMY

You crawl over me
as I'm fixed
to the floor,
flat as roadkill.

You find
the scene hilarious,
clambering over
this immobile Mommy log.

There is a
dark humor to it—
you have your little bottle,
Mommy has hers.

You sit and smile
a toothless grin
as bright as the too-loud
bulb burning overhead.

This was great fun—
you seem to say.
Let's do it again,
Alky Mommy!

Not to worry,
wee one,
not to fret.
The lesson has only begun.

BLACK OUT

Brain cells are
like pennies:

some people
hoard them.

Others drop them
on the sidewalk,

like litter,
like chaff.

You can toss them
in a fountain

and make a wish,
hide one under

a teen driver's seat
to ward off

ambulances, death.
Or, like me,

you can use them
to buy something perfect,

something sure:
oblivion.

DIVINATION: DEAD SQUIRREL

Even from a distance,
the squirrel corpse in the road
shrieks of raw gore.

Your skipping step
slows to a cautious pace
at the sight. And yet

you tug me closer,
fret your bang-fringed brow,
bend over the car-racked carnage

as if to unlock a message there.
You, who see auras of color
around strangers' heads,

speak of kind ghosts who sit
at the foot of your bed,
summon animals to you

with only quiet grace—
I could believe it of you:
a reader of entrails.

And if you squint and see
our somber future previewed
in a squirrel neatly unzipped

from chin to tail,
you do not love the world
any less—no, no, not yet.

Turning away to skip again,
you say, *He was running
from something chasing him.*

He was trying to get away.

TO A DAUGHTER WITH FINE NEW TEETH

Decluttering a drawer,
a pill bottle rolls, rattling its contents.

Inside—tiny bits of yellowing bone,
fragile as milk glass.

I don't remember keeping your baby teeth,
but of course I did: they came from your small,

still-precious mouth, caused days of anguish
coming in, fits of tears coming out.

Stem cells harvested from these fragments
might one day mend broken genes.

I peer inside an incisor, a tiny kaleidoscope of hope,
see the black remnants of decaying nerve.

If I put this small tooth on my tentative tongue,
would I taste the germ of forgiveness?

I return the teeth to their plastic tomb
and throw them away.

You have new teeth now, and sharp ones.
You are fed, and fat, and free.

GHAZAL: TO A WILD CHILD GROWN

How often did I augur it: the misery of chasing you
down corridors of rottenstone that turned to dust, erasing you?

How countless were those phantom doors that led to you, but there within:
a kneeling man with chalk in hand, his forehead lowered, tracing you.

These fears came early; you were drawn to risk and peril from the start:
a burning candle, busy roads—my days were spent outpacing you.

The willful child grew wanton wings and flew to each temptation posed—
AWOL on drugs, withdrawn from life, the bait of boys, debasing you.

What need would draw you, sure as breath, to crave all things precarious,
although you knew the sure outcome: the weight of guilt, disgracing you?

An unkind god has engineered innate seduction, cellular,
that draws its dupes to sure defeat—the denouement, unlacing you.

My Fulton blood transferred that trait—long lineage of lustful souls
who, though the curse wrought their despair, surround you now, embracing you.

WHAT A MOTHER DOES

1.
Summoned
by a husband's cry
to your pink room.
There:
a pale statue
on the cold floor.
Face cement-hued,
lips of eggplant skin.
At your fingertips:
plunger, tube, needle.
Dot of blood
below its tip:
a grisly
exclamation point,
punctuating
the end of life
as we knew it.

2.
Death
wooed you;
you found him
charming.
He lay atop you
and sucked the
life out of you,
like cats
stealing the breath
of babies
in old wives' tales.

3.
I had imagined
a thousand ways
for you to die

swimming pool kidnapper allergy tornado bee sting
school shooting electric shock forgotten seatbelt
choking hit-and-run carbon monoxide.

But this death
I did not foresee,
could not prevent,
could only hope
to undo—
a kite flyer
doggedly chasing
a runaway string.

4.
I breathe
life into you,
your chest
rises, falls,
but the brittle watch
of your pulse
strives
for silence.
I exhale again
into the
stilled bags
of your lungs,
praying
they will
snatch up life
like a lost button
sucked into a vacuum's
ravenous throat.

5.
Now:
eyelids flutter,
an enraptured smile
curves your
pinkening lips.

Then horror:
your eyes open,
point in opposite directions—
one looks at me,

the other at the demon
you adore.

6.
You were dead
and then you weren't.

7.
This is what
a mother does.

EATING DINNER, AFTER YOU DIED

After Pieter Bruegel's "The Fall of Icarus"
and W.H. Auden's "Musée des Beaux Arts"

Just hours ago, I found you ashen and cold
on the floor of your sun-swaddled room,
the needle beside you as splendid in design,
as lethal in misuse, as Icarus's waxed wings.

I did not witness your fall from grace,
only hurried to a thud, as Daedalus no doubt
harkened to a splash—such innocent sounds,
onomatopoeias, merry in the mouths of children.

I lent you lungsful of my half-used breath,
swallowing fury and fear like poisoned prayers,
waiting for sirens to turn up our street,
to turn back time in a miraculous reanimation.

Now, you sit beside me and sip soup off a spoon
with your pink-again lips, swallow, stare at the TV—
at raging fires, caged children, the shot-dead,
the turned-away—then sip, swallow, stare again.

Even you, so newly scolded by the sun after
aiming for an ecstasy not meant for this earth—
your white legs disappearing into deep oblivion—
even you quite leisurely turn away from disaster.

Did Daedelus learn something about hubris
as he watched his son plummet into the laughing sea?
And what am I to learn from this echo of error?
I crafted your wings from my own blood and hours.

Tomorrow, the untroubled world will resume:
the ploughman will walk dully behind his horse,
expensive, delicate ships will hoist their sails,
the fisherman will gaze lazily at a tug on his line.

And only the fish ripped gasping from the sea,
the whipped horse, the scurvy-ridden sailor,
the mother who wrestled Thanatos and now faces blame,
will glimpse something startling and not turn away.

THE WAITINGS

I'm listening for the ambulance,
listening with a heart pumping
hard enough to flood both
our brains with oxygen
as I share my breath with you,
the way we used to share
blankets at the beach, a single chair.

For a moment, you're five again,
and we're awaiting the bus
on your first day of school,
you in your pressed cotton dress
and Little Mermaid backpack,
pink glasses glinting in sunlight,
the dog sitting by your side
at the end of the asphalt driveway,
and all I can think is that
if you step forward too soon,
you'll be bulldozed by inattention,
souped-up speed, sun-blindedness,
and all your innocence
will pour out under those
chrome-capped kill wheels.

You're breathing on your own now;
your lips bloom the color
of cabbage roses on dusty wallpaper,
enlivening the indigo pods
that withered there when
my mouth first covered yours
like a sloppy, school-boy kiss.

There is hope in this pink room,
but I know that the needle
beside you on the floor
has an army of brothers
as close as the closet,
as distant as yesterday,
as innumerable as stars
in a black sky.

Now the doorbell rings
and the school bus arrives,
yellow and alive,
screeching to a stop,
waiting for you.

DUPLEX: BROKEN GENES

after Jericho Brown

Her life was once as soft as shattered glass,
a needle and a pipe her only loves.

She promised: no cruel lovers in our home,
but lips of addicts always mutter lies.

When addicts lie, their mothers' ears hear truth.
The truth is this: lies whisper through our genes.

Oblivion is grace, my broken genes proclaimed.
Obedient, she sought my promised path.

The path I promised all my drunken years
was potholed with dark demons, bearing death.

I could not bear her death when demons came;
I shared my breath to bring her back to life.

I brought her back to life to start again.
Our future is as clear as shattered glass.

REHAB

This fine, safe place
where the poison
slowly drains from you,
where you are awash
in spells and mumbo jumbo,
where others like you
trade pain for solace,
then solace for pain,
where you listen, night and day,
to nightmares and tears,
where therapists assure you
bad parenting is at fault,
where you dream of using
only to wake to a sweat
of equal parts loathing and longing,
where the movies are screened
for the requisite happy ending,
where we visit you like strangers,
playacting a happy family,
where the placebo of hope
suspends disbelief—

This fine, safe place
has only one door,
and where you came in,
you will go out,
and the person you were
you very much still are.

So pack away their parables
in your safest, deepest pocket,
because the world is an electric chair
of expectation, a drum beat loudly
to drown out too-sweet songs.

CUTTING WITH SPOONS

If my mother's hand had trembled as she spooned
codeine-laced cough syrup into my mouth,

if candy-red droplets had splattered the bedsheet,
spilled vampiric blood, would I have known to fear

her rock-steady hand? Instead, I swallowed
her offered cure, gasped awake for hours,

oxygen-starved, my lungs hypnotized
to stillness by her spoonful of suffocation.

Years later, unrolling a rug from the room
where you injected an overture to death,

I found a spoon, blackened, burnt, its handle
bent back toward the bowl—an absurd remake

of the baby spoon, loop-handled and yellow,
with which you often gagged yourself,

greedily scarfing applesauce, oatmeal, some
innocuous pap from your highchair bowl.

How cruel these spoons, slyly cradling
poison in the guise of benign utility.

They reflect our images upside-down—
how could we miss such a warning?

TO ANOTHER ADDICT'S MOTHER

Waiting is a mother's art;
we do it well. Time does not
melt in our mouths.

Through winters and falls,
full moons, snow, ground
too frozen to dig, we wait.

In spring, we plant flowers,
hide a black dress in the back
of the closet, wait.

We wait in summer,
thinking how soft the ground
will be for them, how warm.

Lightning never strikes twice
the well-wishers say, but we've seen
its blinding blue light. So we wait.

Wait for the knock, the ring,
the siren, the silence,
for the sympathetic voice,

for the man with his hat in his hand,
for the white-coated woman
shaking her head.

Our hearts are water balloons
in a roomful of needles.
What can there be but agony?

We read books, cook dinners,
smile for the camera, knit,
refill our husbands' pill cases.

If wait-time were a currency,
we'd own the seas; if it were fire,
there'd be only scorched earth.

WHAT IT'S LIKE TO BE AN ADDICT'S MOTHER

In Taos Pueblo,
there stands
an ancestral home
that no descendant
has returned to claim.

It melts in rain and snow,
red-clay adobe dissolving
into the earth
like the blood
of a felled sacred deer.

This is what it's like
to be an addict's mother:
linoleum scuffed
colorless under
an anxious child's chair,

the gradual attrition
of substance
from sweaters
tossed too often
in the dryer's heat.

A thing
disappearing,
unclaimed,
worn to
nothingness,
abased.

THE RELAPSE

Mated swans build their nests
atop sedges piled high in shallow water,
far from the shore where predators teem.

But in flooding rains, fast-rising water
can threaten the clutch. Toil as they may
to elevate their grass-lined cradle,

the swans sometimes fail. And when
no exertion can avert ruin—submersion—
the cob and pen simply swim away.

Ornithologists defend the birds' desertion
as the instinctive expectation of future broods.
But I judged them heartless.

When you relapsed, we delivered you home
to the pillowed comfort of the couch. Day and night,
we guarded you from texts, temptation, flight.

On the third morning, withdrawal ravaged
your brain, and every molecule of you wailed.
You fell to your knees and begged:

Please, Mommy, please—if you love me,
let me go just one more time. I labored
to raise you, to lift you from the flood,

but peering down into your face,
eons of instinct whispered
swim away.

Photo: *Swim Away*, by Chuck Jennes

THE FEATHERED THING

after Emily Dickinson

When it perched in my soul,
I fed it sharp seeds of despair.
When it stopped singing,
I doused it with 80 proof.
When its feathers fell out,
I raged, forgetting I plucked
each quill, like hairs ripped
from my own sodden scalp.

How many times did I
revive that poor, naked bird
with breaths of false resolve,
only to abash it again?

Through sore gale and
strange sea, I pecked away
at nothingness.
It tasted like life.

Finally, I fell to my knees,
begged the bird's return.

For years, I've held
the cage door open.
Now and then,
the feathered thing
flits in and out again,
too wary still to stay.

I'll build a nest
of good deeds and poems,
of love given and received.
I'll fashion it a fine home,
a worthy perch.

Then
I'll ask it to sing for me.

WHO IS TO SAY?

We've spent years now, you and I,
piecing our remnants back together,
self-mending with all manner
of metaphoric glue—human *kintsugi*,
the principles of pottery applied to flesh,
hoping to make our fractured seams gleam.

Who is to say,
who is to say which would be lovelier:
what we are now
or our might-have-been bowls?

Wabi-sabi:
the poetic find beauty in imperfection.
But pragmatic potters like us,
we just want the soup not to leak.

TRIPLE HELIX

Her sorrow, my sorrow, your sorrow:
a braid of bad things runs long
down our backs, tumbles down generations
like a Slinky toy on the stairs.

She dulled her despair with dirt,
sunlight in her eyes, a garden
of growing things. But in winter
she was a dead leaf, tossed and dragged

by every feckless wind. You and I
opted for year-round solutions to quell
the gloom gurgling through our veins;
our pacifiers offered oblivion on demand.

Now she is gone, buried in the dirt
that once dissipated her darkness.
You and I are left to untangle the necklace
left behind in her joyless box of jewels.

Daughter, let's pry apart the DNA
that twists our fates together,
separate the triple helix of eye color,
child-bearing hips, despondency.

Let's cut our braids and go bald—
brides leaving home for a new village,
leaving behind the chattel of the past,
carrying only our finest things.

RETURN

I awoke thirsty.
Winter left me parched.

Rain nursed me,
swaddled me in fog.

Birds came,
their small feet
lighter than I remembered.

They sang. They flew.
They found others
and brought them to me.

A surge ran through me
like a jolt of lightning
carried through soaked soil.

It was a remembered longing:
for leaves to unfurl
at the very ends of me,

for life to return
after a long night.

HOVENWEEP

Here the Ancient Ones farmed the mesa
atop the rim of a meandering canyon,

carved their homes, their silos, their kivas
into the walls of steep sandstone cliffs.

You and I creep closer to the edge of the maw,
daring to see the crumbled ruins below.

Holding hands, sure each will save the other
if the ledge gives way under our weight,

we smile and take another step, and another.
Even your father calls us back: *Enough.*

But you and I know this ledge-walking well:
we've danced on edges of our own making,

explored paths of exhilaration
no one else could fathom or forgive,

danced alone, as all addicts dance, even
as our dances devolved into madness.

And then you, a damaged daughter, saved me.
And then I, a mother damned, saved you.

Now, the voice of a park ranger, God-like,
calls us back from the precipice.

Grousing, we stumble back, hide our relief.
We did not really want to see how it ended.

CPSIA information can be obtained
at www.ICGtesting.com
Printed in the USA
JSHW042235270822
29667JS00003B/60